W9-CXS-158

YOU ARE MY
FRIENDS

By Ron Wormser, Russ Korth and Ron Wormser Jr.

A Bible Study from

Churches Alive!
MINISTERING TO THE CHURCHES OF THE WORLD
Box 3800, San Bernardino, California 92413

Copyright 1989, Churches Alive International
San Bernardino, California
ISBN 0-934396-42-6

All rights reserved, including translation. No part of
this publication may be reproduced, stored in a
retrieval system, or transmitted in any form or by any
means, electronic, mechanical, photocopy, recording,
or otherwise, without the written permission of the
copyright owner.

Published by Churches Alive International.
Churches Alive is a non-profit organization. Gifts for
the purpose of helping this ministry serve the local
church are tax deductible.

Printed in the United States of America.

Scripture quotations are taken from the HOLY BIBLE;
NEW INTERNATIONAL VERSION, copyright 1978,
by the New York International Bible Society,
used by permission of Zondervan Bible Publishers.

C O N T E N T S

The writing team of Ron Wormser, Russ Korth and Ron Wormser Jr. has collaborated on more than 15 books for small groups. They authored the *Love One Another* and *God in You* Bible study series which have sold one million copies.

As staff members of Churches Alive, these men have worked side by side with church leaders and in small groups across the country. They have combined their insights to create effective small group experiences such as the book you hold in your hands.

Ron Wormser was formerly a radio speaker and pastor and served as National Coordinator of the Lay Ministry and Director of Mass Media for Campus Crusade for Christ.

Russ Korth previously was staff member with the Navigators where he served as an area and regional director and as Director of Materials Development.

Ron Wormser Jr. was production manager and director for a television station and led the discipling ministry of a growing church.

Jesus was a friendly person. He spent time with people, came to their homes, ate with them, answered their questions, healed them, cared for them. He was available day and night to people's ideas, questions and needs.

Jesus formed friendships with some unexpected people. Few were religious. Many were common folks — businessmen, merchants, craftsman. Others were scoundrels, cheaters and even women of low repute. Certainly an unusual collection of friends.

But Jesus wasn't a close friend with everyone. He said, "You are my friends if you do what I command you." To become a close friend of Jesus, many of these people had to make changes. They had to begin to practice what they learned from him.

In the chapters of this book, you will meet some of Jesus' friends. You will learn how they became his friends and how you can follow their example to become a better friend with him. And, as you deepen your friendship with Jesus, you will also deepen your friendships with others who are drawing close to him.

This book is not like most other books. It is designed to help you experience friendship, not just read about it. As you go through these pages, don't rush ahead looking for more knowledge -- enjoy the experiences that are designed for you. Play the games. Give your answers. Express your opinions and feelings. Engage in relaxed discussion. Be a friend.

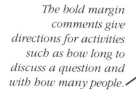

The bold margin comments give directions for activities such as how long to discuss a question and with how many people.

The lighter margin comments shed light on portions of the Bible passage.

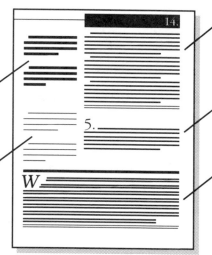

The scripture passage is provided to make it easy to enjoy the activities and discussion.

The numbered activities are questions to discuss, role playing, games and other exercises.

Each chapter includes a paragraph that ends in the focus statement for your group meeting.

CHAPTER ONE

ZACCHAEUS

Jesus Seeks You Out.

Someone should read the introduction on page five aloud.

*W*hen Jesus came to Jericho, he was greeted by crowds of people who came to view this great teacher and healer. In spite of the confusion and the press of the crowd, Jesus sought out a person he wanted to spend some time with. In the same way, Jesus seeks you out.

Discuss questions 1 and 2 in groups of four people, for 10 minutes.

1. Introduce yourself to your group by telling your name and where you grew up.

2. As you were growing up, who was one of your best friends?

What is one of the most memorable incidents you had with this friend?

When did you begin to see Jesus as your friend?

Luke 19:1-10

¹Jesus entered Jericho and was passing through. ²A man was there by the name of Zacchaeus; he was a chief tax collector and was wealthy. ³He wanted to see who Jesus was, but being a short man he could not, because of the crowd. ⁴So he ran ahead and climbed a sycamore-fig tree to see him, since Jesus was coming that way.

⁵When Jesus reached the spot, he looked up and said to him, "Zacchaeus, come down immediately. I must stay at your house today." ⁶So he came down at once and welcomed him gladly.

⁷All the people saw this and began to mutter, "He has gone to be the guest of a 'sinner.'"

⁸But Zacchaeus stood up and said to the Lord, "Look, Lord! Here and now I give half of my possessions to the poor, and if I have cheated anybody out of anything, I will pay back four times the amount."

⁹Jesus said to him, "Today salvation has come to this house, because this man, too, is a son of Abraham. ¹⁰For the Son of man came to seek and to save what was lost."

Come back together into one group. Someone should read the passage aloud.

(Verses 1, 2) Jericho was a central collecting station for taxes for the surrounding region. The chief tax collector often sold the right to collect taxes to the highest bidder. Those who bought the right to collect taxes could then levy additional fees on citizens as they wished.

(Verse 8) The reputation of most tax collectors was clouded by their thievery and improprieties. Zacchaeus' statement, "If I have cheated anybody," was not a defense of his innocence, but another way of saying he would make restitution.

3. To understand this incident better, it helps to know more about Zacchaeus. What are all the things we know about him from this passage?

The leader should write responses to question 3 on the chalkboard.

4. As you look at the list, in what ways do you identify with Zacchaeus? In what ways do you feel you are different?

Form groups of four and discuss questions 5 and 6 for a total of 15 minutes. Every person in your group should participate.

5. Have you ever seen a famous person in a parade or a procession? Who did you see?

If that person stopped the parade, turned to you and asked to come to your house, how would you react?

☐ Oh, no! My house is a mess!
☐ If only my friends could see me now!
☐ I can't believe this is happening!
☐ I hope my kids don't embarrass me.
☐ I would act like he was talking to someone else.

6. What excuses could Zacchaeus have given for not accepting Jesus' invitation?

What excuses do people give today for not responding to Jesus?

Discuss the rest of the chapter as a whole group.

7. Zacchaeus didn't offer excuses. He gladly had Jesus in his home. Why do you think he welcomed Jesus?

8. What do you think Jesus meant when he said to Zacchaeus, "Today salvation has come to this house"?

9. What elements of beginning a friendship do you see in this event?

The leader should list responses to questions 9 and 10 on the chalkboard.

Look through the list you just made. How do these elements help you to relate to Jesus as your friend?

10. In what ways do you see that Jesus has sought you out?

Zacchaeus was not the only person with whom Jesus wanted to spend extra time. This was typical of Jesus. He wanted to reach everybody. And Jesus seeks a relationship with you -- a relationship that begins with knowing him as the way to life and grows into a warm friendship

Beginning with the leader, each person should complete the sentence, "A friend is _____" in a meaningful way.

SIMON AND THE FORGIVEN WOMAN

Jesus accepts you.

*J*esus once attended a dinner party at the house of a religious leader. During the course of the evening, the unthinkable happened — a prostitute showed up. Even worse, she began to make a scene in showing her love and gratitude to Jesus. But one of the great things about Jesus is that he accepts you, no matter who you are or what you've done.

Some one should read the passage aloud.

(verse 37) Custom at this time allowed for people to come uninvited to this kind of dinner. These guests would sit against the walls and could converse with the people at the table.

(verse 38) Dinner guests ate in a reclining position around a low table. This allowed the woman to be behind Jesus at his feet. To the Jews, a woman letting down her hair in public was a shameful thing.

(verse 41) The denarius, a Roman silver coin, was worth about a day's wages.

Luke   7:36-50

36Now one of the Pharisees invited Jesus to have dinner with him, so he went to the Pharisee's house and reclined at the table. 37When a woman who had lived a sinful life in that town learned that Jesus was eating at the Pharisee's house, she brought an alabaster jar of perfume, 38and as she stood behind him at his feet weeping, she began to wet his feet with her tears. Then she wiped them with her hair, kissed them and poured perfume on them.

39When the Pharisee who had invited him saw this, he said to himself, "If this man were a prophet, he would know who is touching him and what kind of woman she is — that she is a sinner."

40Jesus answered him, "Simon, I have something to tell you."

"Tell me, teacher," he said.

41"Two men owed money to a certain money-lender. One owed him five hundred denarii, and the other fifty. 42Neither of them had the money to pay him back, so he canceled the debts of both. Now which of them will love him more?"

⁴³Simon replied, "I suppose the one who had the bigger debt canceled."

"You have judged correctly," Jesus said.

⁴⁴Then he turned toward the woman and said to Simon, "Do you see this woman? I came into your house. You did not give me any water for my feet, but she wet my feet with her tears and wiped them with her hair. ⁴⁵You did not give me a kiss, but this woman, from the time I entered, has not stopped kissing my feet. ⁴⁶You did not put oil on my head, but she has poured perfume on my feet. ⁴⁷Therefore, I tell you, her many sins have been forgiven — for she loved much. But he who has been forgiven little loves little."

⁴⁸Then Jesus said to her, "Your sins are forgiven."

⁴⁹The other guests began to say among themselves, "Who is this who even forgives sins?"

⁵⁰Jesus said to the woman, "Your faith has saved you; go in peace."

(verse 44) The host usually provided water and towels for footwashing, since people wore sandals and the streets were dusty.

"You Bet Your Pharisee" — Choose two contestant teams of three people each. The rest of the group becomes the cheering section. The group leader serves as game show host.

The host reads the first question and allows one team to confer and give an answer. The host then reads the second question and allows the other team to answer. High score wins. (Answers are on page 14.)

Play this game to help you learn more about Pharisees.

1. True or False: The Pharisees were a religious and political party in Palestine at the time of Christ.

2. True or False: The Pharisees got their name because of their great emphasis on fairness.

3. True or False: The Pharisees strictly obeyed all the ritual laws, but because of their greed, they did not tithe.

4. True or False: The Pharisees got their name because they organized the first Palestine State Fair.

5. True or False: The Pharisees limited their contact with other Jews and Gentiles because they were not careful to obey their laws and might defile the Pharisees.

6. True or False: The Pharisees were so named because they were a strain of blond, blue-eyed Jews whose skin was very fair.

7. True or False: The Pharisees were aristocrats and were unpopular among the Jews.

8. True or False: The Pharisees got their name because they also drove taxi chariots and charged stiff fares.

Tiebreaker: The Pharisees had their roots in what group of faithful Jews?

Discuss questions 1-3 in groups of four. Spend no more than 15 minutes. Every person in your group should participate.

1. Why do you think Simon, the Pharisee, invited Jesus to dinner? Explain your answer.

☐ He wanted to be seen with a famous person.
☐ He wanted to engage Jesus in a discussion to prove him wrong.
☐ He was curious about who Jesus was and what he was teaching.
☐ He was sincerely interested in hearing more of Jesus' message.
☐ He was planning a dinner party anyway and thought Jesus would make conversation interesting.

2. We don't know the woman's name, but we know she was a prostitute whose heart was touched by Jesus. To understand her better, who do you think were her friends? What do you think the townspeople and the religious people thought of her?

3. The woman demonstrated her deep affection for Jesus. She must have been sobbing for some time to be able to wash Jesus' feet. If you had been in Jesus' situation, would you have allowed the woman to wash your feet? Why or why not?

Why do you think Simon felt as he did?

What do you think the other guests were thinking?

4. The woman used her tears to show her feelings toward Jesus. What do you have with you right now to show how you feel about Jesus? For example, a key ring might show that Jesus opens doors in your life.

Discuss questions 4 and 5 with the entire group.

5. If you were to cast people for the movie version of this event, whom would you cast as Simon, the Pharisee? As the woman?

6. Simon doubted Jesus because Jesus allowed the woman's actions. But Jesus showed that he not only knew the woman's character and need, but also could perceive Simon's thoughts. Jesus told a story to explain the situation. By what he said, do you consider yourself forgiven little or forgiven much? Why?

Return to your group of four to discuss questions 6-8 for the remaining time.

7. Jesus summed up the woman's actions toward him by saying "Her many sins have been forgiven — for she loved much." Then he added, "Your faith has saved you; go in peace." What is the relationship between actions and faith in your friendship with Jesus?

8. What would you say is the main point of this event? Explain your answer.

☐ Loving much
☐ Forgiving
☐ Accepting people with diverse backgrounds
☐ Dinner etiquette
☐ Being a good host
☐ Being perceptive to needs

*T*hrough this event in his life, Jesus showed his great acceptance of people. He accepted Simon's invitation to his house regardless of his motives. He accepted the love and faith of a woman with a sinful past. And Jesus offers you acceptance — an invitation to be his friend.

You Bet Your Pharisee Answers:
1. True
2. False
3. False, tithing was one law they especially emphasized.
4. False
5. True
6. False
7. False, they were often commoners and were respected by the Jews for their religious effort.
8. False, Pharisees means "separated ones."
Tiebreaker: Their roots were in Hasidim (or Chasidin). If still tied after this question, the team with the most dental fillings wins.

MARTHA AND MARY

Jesus Wants To Spend Time With You.

S he was trying her very best. Jesus was in her home and she wanted everything to be just right, but her preparations distracted her from hearing what Jesus had to say. Gently, but clearly, Jesus told Martha to calm down. Just as with Martha, Jesus wants to spend time with you.

Luke   10:38-42

Someone should read the passage aloud.

38 As Jesus and his disciples were on their way, he came to a village where a woman named Martha opened her home to him. 39 She had a sister called Mary, who sat at the Lord's feet listening to what he said. 40 But Martha was distracted by all the preparations that had to be made. She came to him and asked, "Lord, don't you care that my sister has left me to do the work by myself? Tell her to help me!"

41 "Martha, Martha," the Lord answered, "you are worried and upset about many things, 42 but only one thing is needed. Mary has chosen what is better, and it will not be taken away from her."

(verse 40) Martha was probably the older sister and head of the household. As such, she was responsible for housekeeping and hostessing.

1. If Jesus was coming to stay at your house, what are the three most important things you would do to prepare for his visit? (Your group should decide on the three most important things.)

When you're ready, tell the other group what you decided.

Divide your group with all the men in one group, and all the women in the other. Take five minutes to discuss question 1.

Form groups of four and spend no more than 15 minutes discussing questions 2 through 4.

2. The Bible indicates that it wasn't just Jesus, but also his disciples who came to Martha's home. She was caught in a flurry of preparation. She probably didn't have much warning before all these guests arrived. What are the good things you see in Martha?

3. Mary "sat at the Lord's feet listening to what he said." Why do you think Mary didn't help Martha?

☐ She didn't feel it was her responsibility.
☐ She thought Martha could handle things alone.
☐ She didn't realize Martha needed help.
☐ She could never please Martha anyway, so why try?
☐ She didn't feel the preparations were necessary.
☐ She intended to help, but got caught up in conversation.

4. Jesus probably surprised Martha when he told her to calm down. Why do you think Jesus took Mary's side?

☐ He didn't think Martha's preparations were necessary.
☐ He didn't want anyone to make a fuss over him.
☐ He was saying some very important things and Martha was distracting people with her busyness.
☐ He thought they should talk first and get dinner and beds ready later.

Come back together as a whole group.

5. In responding to Martha, the Lord said that, "Mary has chosen what is better." How, like Martha, are you doing good things, but could be choosing "what is better"?

6. Though the story says nothing about Martha's response, what do you think Martha did after Jesus told her to relax and spend some time with him?

☐ Apologized, found an inconspicuous place to sit down and listened attentively.

☐ Finished doing a few of the more important things, and then listened while standing in a doorway near the kitchen so she could attend to the food.

☐ Kept working, angry at Mary.

☐ Sat down to listen, but kept thinking about all the things that needed doing.

7. One way I'm like Martha...........

One way I'm like Mary..............

8. In your group, make a list of what you like to do when entertaining guests, what you don't like to do when entertaining and what you wished the other group understood about you.

Give a brief report to the other group on your anwers.

Divide into two groups, those who feel they are most like Martha and those who feel they are most like Mary. Discuss question 8 for five minutes.

9. What has helped you to spend time with Jesus?

If you could change one thing about the time you spend with Jesus, what would it be?

Come back together as a whole group.

F riendships are usually built over time as people share their ideas, hopes, dreams and experiences with one another. Developing a friendship with Jesus is much the same.

CHAPTER FOUR

LEVI
Jesus Offers A Better Life.

Years ago, Jesus met a shrewd businessman who was working to get ahead. He was probably not unlike many business people who greatly value the comforts and rewards that accompany success. But this businessman learned that Jesus offers a better life.

If your group is larger than six people, divide into smaller groups for the following game.

"Things I've Never Done" — Give everyone six $1,000 bills of play money. Go around the circle trying to name one thing you have never done that you think everyone else in your group has done. The people who have done what you name must give you one of their bills. Those who have not done what you name may keep their money. After you have gone around the circle two times, everyone should count their money to see who has gained the most.

In playing this game, many people soon learn how to be cunning in order to get ahead, but Levi would have won this game. That's the kind of person it took to be a tax collector.

Someone should read the passage aloud.

(Verse 27) Levi is also called "Matthew" for whom the first Gospel is named. His tax booth was probably located along a main road to collect duty on goods transported by that road.

Luke   5:27-32

27 After this, Jesus went out and saw a tax collector by the name of Levi sitting at his tax booth. "Follow me," Jesus said to him, 28 and Levi got up, left everything and followed him.

29 Then Levi held a great banquet for Jesus at his house, and a large crowd of tax collectors and others were eating with them. 30 But the Pharisees and

the teachers of the law who belonged to their sect complained to his disciples, "Why do you eat and drink with tax collectors and 'sinners'?"

³¹ Jesus answered them, "It is not the healthy who need a doctor, but the sick. ³² I have not come to call the righteous, but sinners to repentance."

(Verse30) The Pharisees limited their contact with other people, including other Jews. They could not eat in the homes on a non-Pharisee because they could not be sure the laws of ritual purity and tithing of the food had been maintained.

1. What are some things people think they must give up for God?

Discuss questions 1 and 2 with the whole group. The leader should write the responses on a chalk-board.

2. What do you think caused Levi to leave all for Jesus?

☐ His riches left him empty.
☐ He had a sincere religious conviction.
☐ He saw the potential of a life with Jesus.
☐ God zapped him.

3. Role play a conversation between Jesus and Levi. One of you take the role of Jesus and the other of Levi. As Jesus, tell why Levi should walk away from it all. As Levi, tell why it is tough for you to walk away. If there is still time, reverse roles and play it again.

Choose a partner and spend five minutes in the role play situation in question 3.

4. After leaving his tax collecting booth, Levi threw a big party for Jesus. What kind of party would you hold if Jesus was coming to your house, and why?

Now form groups of four and discuss questions 4 and 5 for 15 minutes.

☐ An intimate dinner party
☐ An elaborate, catered event, complete with waiters
☐ A back yard barbecue
☐ A pot luck
☐ A "thanksgiving dinner"
☐ A "regular" family meal

What are the names of other people you would invite to your party?

5. Tax collectors and Pharisees generally had two distinct lifestyles. Below is a list of some of the qualities that were associated with each of them. Place a checkmark next to the qualities that you identify with.

Pharisee
- ☐ Disciplined
- ☐ Detail oriented
- ☐ Loyal
- ☐ Scholarly
- ☐ Traditional
- ☐ Upright
- ☐ Uncompromising
- ☐ Popular
- ☐ Idealistic

Tax Collector
- ☐ Enterprising
- ☐ Unconventional
- ☐ Practical
- ☐ Realistic
- ☐ Party goers
- ☐ Risk taking
- ☐ Affluent
- ☐ Industrious
- ☐ Clever

Count your checkmarks above to see which type of person you are most like and discuss your reactions in your group

Come back together as a whole group.

6. Some of the leading citizens of the community were critical of Jesus forming friendships with corrupt people like Levi and his friends. Jesus' response is found in verses 31 and 32. In his response, who do you think are the healthy? The sick? The righteous? The sinners?

7. As a doctor offers a better life to a sick person, what kind of better life does Jesus offer?

8. Levi physically left his occupation and place of business to follow Jesus. He continued to follow Jesus by traveling with him. In what sense do you feel Jesus is calling you to follow him?

9. Levi saw his business as an obstacle to developing a close relationship with Jesus. Which of the following may be an obstacle between you and a closer relationship with Jesus:

On your own, take several minutes to think about question 9.

☐ An unwillingness to be honest with myself
  (1 John 1:7-9)
☐ An attitude of self-sufficiency (Proverbs 3:5,6)
☐ Resistance to change (Isaiah 45:9)
☐ Fear of rejection by my friends (1 Peter 4:2-4)
☐ Placing too much value on my possessions
  (Matthew 6:19-21)

Spend time this week reflecting on the verse(s) that corresponds to the item you checked above. Ask God to give you insight and application for a better life.

When Levi left his tax collection business, it is unlikely he had a clear concept of all that was in store for him. Yet, in spite of this uncertainty, he knew enough about Jesus to know that he offered a better life. Levi continued to follow Jesus and became one of Jesus' closest friends. Despite the hardships he encountered as a friend of Jesus, Levi never returned to his old way of life.

CHAPTER FIVE

A FATHER WITH FAITH

You Can Begin With Small Faith.

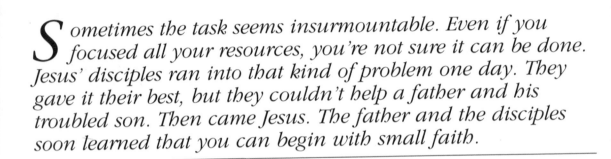

*S*ometimes the task seems insurmountable. Even if you focused all your resources, you're not sure it can be done. Jesus' disciples ran into that kind of problem one day. They gave it their best, but they couldn't help a father and his troubled son. Then came Jesus. The father and the disciples soon learned that you can begin with small faith.

Divide into groups of four and spend five minutes playing the game and five minutes discussing the concluding question.

"Baloney" - One person in the group should make an outlandish statement that may or may not be true. Other group members should indicate whether they doubt the statement or believe it by saying "baloney" or "no baloney." Take turns making statements. Each person should have at least three turns. Keep score on how often you guess correctly.

How is the faith you had in people's answers like or unlike the faith you should have in God?

Each person in your group should mentally assume one of the roles in the story.

1. Sometimes assuming the role of a person in a passage helps you to understand it. Read the information that corresponds to your role.

Role 1 - The Three Disciples
You're returning from a special time with Jesus. As you join the other disciples, you are still talking about your experience.

Role 2 - The Other Disciples

You're waiting for Jesus and the other three disciples. You encountered an epileptic boy and his father, and tried to heal the boy. Jesus had given you the ability to heal before, but now it "wasn't working." Jesus' detractors are criticizing him and your unsuccessful attempts to heal the boy.

Role 3 - The Father and the Boy

You've heard about the great miracles performed by Jesus and his followers. The demon plaguing your life has given no opportunity for a normal life, because he can afflict you at anytime. Now Jesus' disciples have tried and failed.

Role 4 - The Teachers of the Law

As Jewish religious leaders, you have been sent to gather information about this Jesus, who you feel has been misleading the people. You catch his disciples attempting and failing to cast out a demon.

Mark 9:14-27

14 When they came to the other disciples, they saw a large crowd around them and the teachers of the law arguing with them. 15 As soon as all the people saw Jesus, they were overwhelmed with wonder and ran to greet him.

16 "What are you arguing with them about?" he asked.

17 A man in the crowd answered, "Teacher, I brought you my son, who is possessed by a spirit that has robbed him of speech. 18 Whenever it seizes him, it throws him to the ground. He foams at the mouth, gnashes his teeth and becomes rigid. I asked your disciples to drive out the spirit, but they could not."

19 "O unbelieving generation," Jesus replied, "how long shall I stay with you? How long shall I put up with you? Bring the boy to me."

20 So they brought him. When the spirit saw

Someone should read the passage aloud. As the passage is read, view the events through the eyes of the people whose role you assumed.

(verse 14) The teachers of the law were approved to interpret and apply the religious law of the Jews

Jesus, it immediately threw the boy into a convulsion. He fell to the ground and rolled around, foaming at the mouth.

²¹ Jesus asked the boy's father, "How long has he been like this?"

"From childhood," he answered. ²² "It has often thrown him into fire or water to kill him. But if you can do anything, take pity on us and help us."

²³ " 'If you can'?" said Jesus. "Everything is possible for him who believes."

²⁴ Immediately the boy's father exclaimed, "I do believe; help me overcome my unbelief!"

²⁵ When Jesus saw that a crowd was running to the scene, he rebuked the evil spirit. "You deaf and dumb spirit," he said, "I command you, come out of him and never enter him again."

²⁶ The spirit shrieked, convulsed him violently and came out. The boy looked so much like a corpse that many said, "He's dead." ²⁷ But Jesus took him by the hand and lifted him to his feet, and he stood up.

(verse 22) In love, the boy's father identifies himself with his son's malady as he begs Jesus, "Take pity on us and help us."

2. As you listened to the passage in the role you assumed, what were you thinking, feeling and doing as the event unfolded?

Continue in your group of four. Since you will be in discussion groups for the rest of your meeting, try to maintain a pace of no more than five minutes per question.

3. Describe a problem you've had that was just too big to handle.

4. When Jesus said, "Oh unbelieving generation, how long shall I stay with you? How long shall I put up with you?" who do you think he was talking to? Explain your answer.

☐ The teachers of the law
☐ The father
☐ The crowd
☐ His disciples

Who are the unbelieving generation today?

5. The boy's father said to Jesus, "If you can do anything..." There are several ways to ask God for something:

"If you can..."
"If you will..."
"Since you already have..."

Which phrase expresses how you most often feel toward God?

Which of the phrases are expressions of faith? Explain.

6. The boy's father said, "I do believe; help me overcome my unbelief!" When, if ever, have you felt like that?

Is this statement a confession of faith or of doubt? Why?

7. What does it mean to you when Jesus said, "Everything is possible."?

☐ You want it? You got it!
☐ It may not be probable, but it might be possible.
☐ Anything's possible if you know the secret.
☐ Anything's possible if Jesus decides to do it.

8. Imagine you were one of the disciples who tried, and failed, to heal the boy; now Jesus has healed him. What would you like to say to the crowd and Pharisees?

Have small labels or stickers for each person in the group.

9. Jesus responded to the father's request and cured the boy. You also probably have a request you would like to have answered by Jesus. On a small label or sticker, write down one thing you would like to have faith to ask of Jesus. Then place the sticker somewhere you will see it every day, to remind you to have faith to ask Jesus for your request. Next week, you will be able to give a report about how this step of faith has affected you, your requests and your faith in Jesus.

A nother Bible writer, in describing this incident, quoted Jesus as saying to his disciples, "If you have faith as small as a mustard seed...nothing will be impossible for you." In Jesus' time, the mustard seed was the smallest seed known. Mustard plants grew wild along the roadsides to a height of 15 feet. In the same way, small faith in Jesus can produce great results.

ANDREW, SIMON PETER, PHILIP AND NATHANAEL

Jesus Sees Your Potential.

Before discussing this chapter, spend several minutes reporting on your faith experiment (question 9 of Chapter Five).

*J*esus chose some unlikely people for friends. But he saw them not only as they were; he saw them as they could be. When Jesus met an emotional, impulsive and unreliable person, Simon, he called him Petra — rock. Just as with Simon, Jesus sees your potential.

Discuss question 1 in groups of four people for seven minutes.

1. Imagine yourself five years in the future. A news reporter is interviewing you. What heading would she write that tells the latest development in your life? (It may be a character change, a career move or some form of service.)

Several people should read the passage aloud by taking the parts of the narrator, John, the two disciples, Jesus, Andrew, Philip and Nathanael.

John 1:35-51

³⁵ The next day John was there again with two of his disciples. ³⁶ When he saw Jesus passing by, he said, "Look, the Lamb of God!"

³⁷ When the two disciples heard him say this,

(verse 35) "John" refers to John the Baptist, whose ministry was to prepare people to receive the Messiah, the deliverer sent from God.

(verse 39) The 10th hour was about 4 p.m.

(verse 42) Cephas (or Peter) means "rock."

they followed Jesus. ³⁸ Turning around, Jesus saw them following and asked, "What do you want?"

They said, "Rabbi" (which means Teacher), "where are you staying?"

³⁹ "Come," he replied, "and you will see."

So they went and saw where he was staying, and spent that day with him. It was about the tenth hour.

⁴⁰ Andrew, Simon Peter's brother, was one of the two who heard what John had said and who had followed Jesus. ⁴¹ The first thing Andrew did was to find his brother Simon and tell him, "We have found the Messiah" (that is, the Christ).⁴² And he brought him to Jesus.

Jesus looked at him and said, "You are Simon son of John. You will be called Cephas" (which, when translated, is Peter).

⁴³ The next day Jesus decided to leave for Galilee. Finding Philip, he said to him, "Follow me."

⁴⁴ Philip, like Andrew and Peter, was from the town of Bethsaida. ⁴⁵ Philip found Nathanael and told him, "We have found the one that Moses wrote about in the Law, and about whom the prophets also wrote — Jesus of Nazareth, the son of Joseph."

⁴⁶ "Nazareth! Can anything good come from there?" Nathanael asked.

"Come and see," said Philip.

⁴⁷ When Jesus saw Nathanael approaching, he said of him, "Here is a true Israelite, in whom there is nothing false."

⁴⁸ "How do you know me?" Nathanael asked.

Jesus answered, "I saw you while you were still under the fig tree before Philip called you."

⁴⁹ Then Nathanael declared, "Rabbi, you are the Son of God; you are the King of Israel."

⁵⁰ Jesus said, "You believe because I told you I saw you under the fig tree. You shall see greater things than that." ⁵¹ He then added, "I tell you the truth, you shall see heaven open, and the angels of God ascending and descending on the Son of Man."

2. The two disciples "spent that day with him.." What do you think they were doing?

Discuss questions 2-3 as a whole group.

If you could physically spend the day with Jesus, what would you do together?

3. The men whom Jesus met that day went on to become some of his closest friends. What do you see in Jesus' contact with the two disciples as a pattern for developing friendships?

4. When Nathanael heard where Jesus was from, he questioned the potential of a person coming from such an out-of-the-way place. People today may respond in the same way to Jesus and his followers. How could you respond in a positive manner to someone who says:

Divide again into groups of three or four. Each group should take one of the statements below and discuss how they might respond in a positive way. Then report back to the whole group after seven minutes.

a. "I don't trust anyone promoted by those TV preachers."
b. "Church people are always fighting about something. I don't much care for their Jesus."
c. "I know a religious family who lost a child in a tragic accident. Is that how Jesus takes care of his people?"
d. "I have enough trouble in my life. I don't need to start hanging around with a bunch of restrictive people."
e. "All those Christians want you for is your money. You'd think God was broke."

Continue in your small groups. Be sure to allow at least 10 minutes to discuss the closing exercise on page 31.

5. Jesus said some positive things to Simon and Nathanael. He renamed Simon "rock," though during Jesus' life on earth, Simon was anything but solid and unwavering. He called Nathanael a "straight shooter." What positive things would you like Jesus to say about you? (Indicate your top three choices. These things don't have to be true of you right now.)

☐ Honest
☐ Understanding
☐ Cheerful
☐ Patient
☐ Gracious
☐ Intelligent

☐ Loyal
☐ Wise
☐ Encouraging
☐ Disciplined
☐ Thoughtful
☐ Giving

6. Jesus is referred to by many different names and titles in this passage. Which of these names best expresses how you feel toward Jesus?

☐ **Lamb of God** — The suffering servant who paid for my sins. The one who made the supreme sacrifice for me.

☐ **Rabbi** — A title of respect meaning "my teacher." The one I look to for instruction and guidance.

☐ **Messiah** —The deliverer from God, to establish his rule. My long-awaited hope.

☐ **Jesus of Nazareth, Son of Joseph** — his "legal" description, identifying his town and family. "Jesus" means "Jehovah is salvation." A real person I can identify with.

☐ **Son of God** — A title given by the angel who announced Jesus' birth to his mother, Mary. My concept of who God is and how God acts.

☐ **Son of Man** — How Jesus most often referred to himself -- one who represents all that I can be. My connection to God.

7. Seeing the worth and potential of people is important to developing good friendships. Here's a chance to express your feelings to people in your group who have made it a special experience. Below is a list of the many people in this book to whom Jesus extended his friendship. Write the name of the person and characteristic that best represents him or her, then let one person sit silently while the others tell where they put that person's name. Repeat this for each of your group of four.

_____ **Zacchaeus**
Inquisitive, spunky and successful. One who is open to change.

_____ **Simon, the Pharisee**
Intellectual, disciplined and popular. A person who is anxious to do his or her best.

_____ **The forgiven woman**
Transparent, trusting and demon strative. someone who is outgoing in their care and concern.

_____ **Martha**
Practical, hard-working and responsible. Someone you can trust to get things done.

_____ **Mary**
Devoted, sensitive and attentive. A person who exudes warmth.

_____ **Levi**
Enterprising, clever and outgoing The life of the party.

_____ **The father with faith**
Determined, merciful and hopeful.
One who moves out on behalf of
others.

_____ **Andrew and Philip**
Aggresively helpful. Someone
who actively spreads good news.

_____ **Simon Peter**
Pioneering, strong and passionate.
A person who is always one step
ahead.

_____ **Nathanael**
An informed straight-shooter.
You know where you stand with
this person.

"Greater love has no one than this, that he lay down his life for his friends. You are my friends if you do what I command." Jesus, in John 15:13-14

There is Help for Your Church
Howard Ball, Churches Alive President

Churches Alive is much more than a publisher. In fact,
our publishing ministry grew from our direct ministry of
personally assisting local churches to receive the benefits
of a biblical concept we call *Growing by Discipling*.

In *There is Help for Your Church*, Howard Ball explains
the philosophy, concepts and principles of discipleship
and how you can apply them in your church to develop
faithful and effective leaders and members.

Prices on page 39.

HELPING YOUR MINISTRY SUCCEED

In your hand you have just one item of a wide range of discipling helps, authored and developed by Churches Alive with one overall, church-centered, biblical concept in mind:

GROWING BY DISCIPLING!

Convinced that the local church is the heart of God's plan for the world, a number of Christian leaders joined in 1973 to form Churches Alive. They saw the need for someone to work hand-in-hand with local churches to help them develop fruitful discipleship ministries.

Today, the ministry of Churches Alive has grown to include personal consulting assistance to church leaders, a variety of discipleship books and materials, and training conferences for clergy and lay people. These methods and materials have proven effective in churches large and small of over 45 denominations.

You can choose from a variety of resources for you and your church.

From their commitment and experience in church ministry, Churches Alive developed the Growing by Discipling plan to help you:

☐   minister to people at their levels of maturity.
☐   equip people for ministry.
☐   generate mature leaders.
☐   perpetuate quality.
☐   balance growth and outreach.

Every part of Growing by Discipling works together in harmony to meet the diverse needs of people — from veteran church members to the newly awakened in Christ. This discipling approach allows you to integrate present fruitful ministries and create additional ones through the new leaders you develop.

GROWING BY DISCIPLING

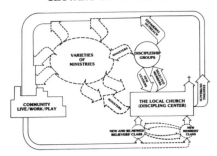

You can develop ministries to expand your effectiveness.

CA staff work with you to develop discipleship ministries that build leaders and faithful ministers for every area of your church ministry.

YOUR CHURCH CAN BENEFIT FROM THE ASSISTANCE OF A CHURCHES ALIVE CONSULTANT

Commitment. Our team of consultants, from varied business and professional backgrounds, are faith missionaries who raise their own support in order to serve your church at the lowest possible cost.

Objectivity. Our staff have an experienced eye in assissing your church's strengths and in developing solutions to your discipling needs.

Vision. A CA consultant can help your leaders gain a vision of how the results of an integrated discipleship program will ripple out to strengthen the entire ministry of your church.

Leadership. Our staff have demonstrated leadership in helping churches devleop an expanding pool of lay leaders.

Results. For more than 15 years, Churches Alive consutlatns have helped churches in 40 states of the United States and 12 countries. You can be confient in their recommendations.

To get in touch with the CA consultant near you, please write or call our headquarters:

**Churches Alive International
Box 3800
San Bernardino, California 92413
(714) 886-5361**

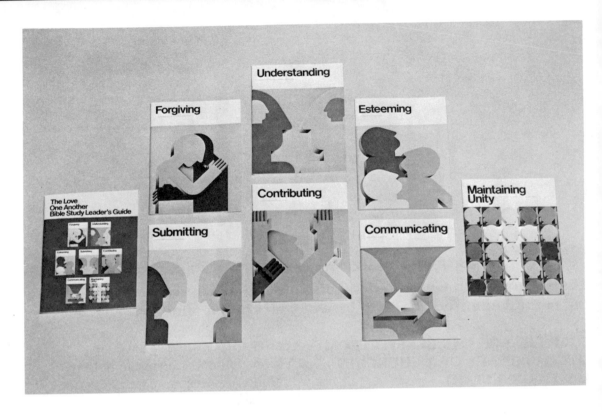

The Love One Another Series

Ron Wormser, Russ Korth & Ron Wormser Jr. with Churches Alive Staff

Improve you personal relationships with these best-selling bible study and discussion guides. Created especially for small groups. The series includes:

Forgiving -- not allowing anything to hinder a relationship.

Understanding -- approaching things from another's point of view.

Esteeming -- holding others in high regard.

Submitting -- allowing God to lead me through others.

Contributing -- helping others fulfill their potential.

Communicating -- conveying truth with love.

Maintaining Unity -- upholding the oneness God gives me with others.

Leader's Guide -- discussion questions, teaching ideas and illustrations.

Prices on page 39.

God in You

Ron Wormser, Russ Korth & Ron Wormser Jr.

Enjoy a passage-oriented approach to Bible study as you discover the tremendous wealth that is yours through God's presence in your life. This series also leads you to develop lifelong Bible study skills you can use with any passage. The series includes:

JESUS! God in you made possible.

ALIVE! God in intimate relationship with you.

RICH! God meeting your deepest needs.

POWERFUL! God enabling you.

CHANGED! Reflecting your love for God.

FULFILLED! Enjoying God's purpose for you.

LEADER'S GUIDE. Perspective, discussion ideas and summaries.

Prices on page 39.

God's Family

Ron Wormser, Russ Korth & Ron Wormser Jr. with Churches Alive Staff

With contemporary word-pictures, attractive graphics and stimulating questions, *God's Family* guides you in uncovering the benefits and responsibilities of being a member of the Church. An excellent entry-level study for new believers and new church members or for focusing veteran Christians on their roles in God's Family. The Leader's Guide Edition includes additional helps for leading discussions in the material.

Prices on page 39.

Lively Discussions!
Russ Korth & Ron Wormser Jr.

Uncork the life in your group. People will appreciate the discussions you generate through good questions. And this book will help you to not only launch discussions, but also to involve everyone in the group, keep things positive, develop trusting relationships and stay on target.

Discussion ideas at the end of each chapter allow you to train group and class leaders to enhance learning through lively discussions.

Prices (Subject to change without notice.)

There is Help for Your Church
Booklet, $2.25
Audio cassette, $4.95

Love One Another
Individual books, $3.50
Leader's Guide for all seven titles, $4.95
Set of all seven titles, $24.50 $20.95 *Save!*

God in You
Special CA prices!
Individual books, $4.95 $4.50
Leader's Guide for all six titles, $5.95 $5.50
Set of all six titles, $29.70 $20.95

Lively Discussions! $5.95
You are My Friends, $3.50

Write or call for a free catalog!

ORDERING FOR YOURSELF?

Your Churches Alive I.D. No.

___ ___ ___ ___ ___ ___
(from previous packing slip or invoice)

Name _____

Address _____
(Street address required for UPS delivery)

_____

City _____ State ___ Zip _____

Phone (_____) _____

ORDERING FOR YOUR CHURCH?

Your Churches Alive I.D. No.

___ ___ ___ ___ ___ ___
(from previous packing slip or invoice)

Your Name _____

Church Name _____

Address _____
(Church street address required for UPS delivery)

City _____ State ___ Zip _____

Phone (_____) _____

Pastor's Name _____

Denomination _____

Qty.	Item	Price Ea.	Total
☐ Please send information about your audio tapes and Discipler's Resource Files.		FREE	
☐ Please send information about your consulting ministry.		FREE	

	Subtotal	
Discounts! Subtract 10% on orders over $40.00 Subtract 15% on orders over $100.00!		
Calif. residents add 6% sales tax		
Postage & Handling		
Total		

Shipping and Handling

All U.S. orders (except Alaska and Hawaii) are shipped via United Parcel Service (UPS), unless otherwise requested. UPS requires a *street* address.

YOUR AREA	SHIPPED VIA	YOUR COST	DELIVERY TIME
1	UPS	4% of subtotal ($1.50 minimum)	3 days
2	UPS	6% of subtotal ($1.50 minimum)	4-6 days
3	UPS	7% of subtotal ($1.50 minimum)	5-7 days
Alaska & Hawaii	Bookpost	3% of subtotal ($1.50 minimum)	2-4 weeks
Canada	Foreign Book Rate	8% of subtotal ($1.50 minimum)	2-4 weeks

☐ Check No. _____ enclosed made payable to **"Churches Alive!"** Foreign checks may not be accepted unless marked "U.S. dollars."

☐ Please charge my ☐ VISA ☐ MasterCard

Account No. _____

Exp. Date _____

Signature _____
(required for charge)

In a Hurry?

We can also ship UPS second day and next day air. There is limited UPS service available for Canada. Phone for details, (714) 886-5361.

Mail To: Churches Alive! Box 3800, San Bernardino, CA 92413

Or for faster delivery, call (714) 886-5361

Satisfaction Guaranteed

If, for any reason, you are not fully satisfied with an item you order, send it back in saleable condition within **60 days** with your invoice or packing slip for a refund (less shipping) or replacement. We'll gladly make the adjustment.

Prices subject to change without notice.